THE·STORY·OF·RELIGION

By BETSY MAESTRO
Illustrated by GIULIO MAESTRO

CLARION BOOKS/New York

In the circle on the title page and cover:

A. BUDDHISM
A 13th-century Buddha from Thailand

B. HINDUISM
A bronze statue of Shiva from the 12th or 13th century

C. JUDAISM
A 1524 Torah depiction of a temple

D. AFRICAN PRIMAL RELIGION
A mask of a deity from Sierra Leone

E. ISLAM
A mosque in Baghdad, Iraq

F. CHRISTIANITY
A saint from a 3rd-century Coptic relief

G. NORTH AMERICAN PRIMAL RELIGION
A Hopi Kachina spirit

Clarion Books
a Houghton Mifflin Company imprint
215 Park Avenue South, New York, NY 10003
Text copyright © 1996 by Betsy Maestro
Illustrations copyright © 1996 by Giulio Maestro

The illustrations for this book were executed in colored pencil, ink, and watercolor.
The text was set in 15/19-point Meridien medium.

For information about this and other Houghton Mifflin trade and reference books
and multimedia products, visit The Bookstore at Houghton Mifflin
on the World Wide Web at (http://www.hmco.com/trade/).

Printed in Hong Kong

Library of Congress Cataloging-in-Publication Data

Maestro, Betsy.
The story of religion / by Betsy Maestro ; illustrated by Giulio Maestro.
p. cm.
ISBN 0-395-62364-2
1. Religions—Juvenile literature. I. Maestro, Giulio. II. Title.
BL92.M27 1995
291—dc20 92-38980
CIP
AC

DNP 10 9 8 7 6 5 4 3

More than five billion people share the planet Earth. The people of the world live in many nations and climates, and have lifeways and languages of amazing variety. The ways people live their lives—the work they do, the foods they eat, the houses they live in—are not the same from place to place, or group to group. In this world, there are many ways of living, speaking, and thinking.

3

Humans spend a good deal of time thinking. All people have ideas and beliefs, but they do not always share the same ideas and beliefs. The things people believe in, the ideas they have, and their ways of looking at the world differ depending on where they live and what group they belong to. Some of the most important human ideas are related to what is called religion. Every religion is made up of a whole set of ideas and beliefs that are so important they often control the way people behave and act.

Many thousands of years ago, humans expressed ideas about their world in cave paintings.

Early people in northern Europe constructed huge stone circles that may have served as astronomical temples.

Religious ideas and beliefs provide answers to questions about the creation of the world, how and why things happen, the meaning of life and death, and what happens to people after they die. Each religion has its own set of answers to these difficult questions. Religious ideas have influenced world history for thousands of years. These powerful beliefs have shaped and controlled the behavior of nations as well as the behavior of individual people.

From the beginning of human history, people have wondered about things they could not understand or explain. Where does the sun go each evening? Why does it rain? What is sleep? Early people were puzzled by these natural occurrences because they did not understand them. Storms, darkness, dreams, and sickness often filled them with dread because they had no control over these events. People wondered who did. They thought that perhaps their world was ruled by unseen forces or powers.

In the Pacific Northwest, Native Americans believed that flashes of lightning came from the eyes and beak of the giant Thunderbird spirit, whose flapping wings caused thunderclaps.

People began to create stories about the events that mystified them. The stories told about the forces or spirits that seemed to control everything in their world. If there was a reason for every happening—if these occurrences could be explained in a way they could understand—then people felt less uncertain. If the spirits were happy, then all would be well, but if the spirits were angered, punishment would surely follow.

An angry river spirit could make floods wash over the land. An angry sun spirit might not return to the sky to bring the light of day. People believed that even the dead had spirits. Since no one knew what happened after death, or what kind of power the dead might possess, people treated the spirits of the dead with respect and appeased them with gifts. If the spirits could be kept happy in their place in the next world, they would not make problems for the living. By pleasing all the spirits, people hoped to be rewarded with a good hunt or a better harvest or fine health.

Early European hunters may have danced to gain power over the spirit of the bear.

In this clay relief from Mesopotamia, in the Middle East, dancers ask the Mother Goddess to send rain.

The spirits were worshiped, obeyed, and thanked for their favors. Ceremonies and rituals were created as ways of communicating with the spirits. Often stories, songs, and dances were part of these ceremonies. The stories explained the creation of the world, the rising and setting of the sun, the dreamworld of sleep, and the next world where dead ancestors dwelled. These stories, ceremonies, and rituals were part of the earliest religions. They gave people a sense of being able to direct the forces that shaped their lives.

A belief in controlling powers in the form of spirits, ghosts, gods, and goddesses was part of all early religions. From the early primitive wanderers to later tribal groups all over the world, people have shared the idea that life was controlled by invisible beings. These people also shared the idea that there was not one but many powerful spirits or gods. A belief in many gods is called polytheism. All early religions were polytheistic. Forms of some of these primal religions are still practiced today.

Most early religions were closely related to nature. People looked to the earth to satisfy their needs. Each aspect of nature—a river, a tree, the soil, a bird, a rock—was represented by a spirit or god. In tribal ceremonies in many places, including Africa and the Americas, masks were worn to represent revered spirits. Stories about these spirits or gods explained changes in nature, such as the phases of the moon and the seasons of the year.

African masks

Sumerian gods

In Sumer, an ancient civilization in the Middle East, people also worshiped many spirits or gods. Every natural force—wind, rain, thunder—was a god. The Sumerians believed that their world was full of these gods of nature, and they carved statues of their likenesses in stone.

Statues of a Sumerian priest and worshipers

The ancient Egyptians also made statues of their gods. They had a strong belief in life after death and constructed elaborate tombs in which they placed the mummified, or carefully preserved, remains of the dead. Since they thought that the dead had the same needs as the living, they provided them with many possessions to carry on to their next life. The ancient Egyptians believed that life on earth was short and unimportant when compared to life after death, which would be eternal or everlasting.

Painted scenes from ancient Egyptian tombs show offerings made to the spirits of the dead.

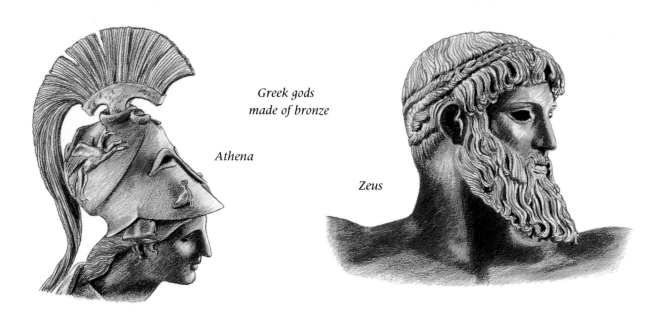

Greek gods
made of bronze

Athena

Zeus

Stories of Greek gods and goddesses are still read today. These myths tell of the adventures of the gods and offer explanations of natural events. The ancient Greeks believed that each element of nature was represented by a different god. However, they didn't think that people needed gods to tell them how to act. The Greeks had a very strong belief in the power and intelligence of the human mind, and felt that people could decide for themselves what was right and what was wrong. Still, they heeded the oracles, or messengers from the gods, who were thought to live on Mount Olympus. Here, Zeus, god of the heavens, was the supreme ruler. The ancient Romans worshiped gods and goddesses very similar to those of the Greeks, although the Romans gave them different names.

Civilizations in the Americas, such as the ancient Maya, also believed in many gods and goddesses. The deities of sun and moon were greatly revered, and calendars and rituals were based on their activities.

Maya gods of
jade and clay

The Maize God

The Sun God

In China, long ago, people also worshiped many gods. Spirits, particularly the ghosts of dead ancestors, were considered worthy of tremendous respect. The Chinese idea of family included not only all living relations, but dead ancestors as well. The Chinese believed that when people died they would become either good or evil spirits. This depended not just on how well they had lived their lives, but also on how well their families cared for them after their deaths.

Many objects were buried in graves to accompany the dead to the Afterworld.

A bird spirit with antlers

A tripod jug and goblet

A clay model of a fancy house

A basket of eggs

A makeup brush and a comb

Carved animal spirits

Later, religion in China changed to become more of a philosophy—a way of thinking about life—and less of a belief in spirits or gods. Many Chinese believe that everything in the world is controlled by two opposite forces. When these forces can be brought into harmony, or balance, good things happen. But when the two forces are at odds, or out of balance, there is discord or disturbance. So the Chinese searched for a way to keep these forces, the Yin and Yang, in accord with each other.

Yin (black) and Yang (white) are circled by eight groups of lines used by priests to guess the wishes of heavenly spirits.

A heavenly dragon disk

Lao Tzu, teacher of the Tao

The Chinese found one answer in Tao. Tao (pronounced *dow*) means "the way." People who follow this way seek to create harmony with nature in all parts of their lives. They see Tao as the force that produces balance in nature and in all the universe. Taoists believe that by observing nature and learning to join with its mysterious force, a person will find peace and fulfillment.

Another answer was the way taught by Confucius (K'ung Fu-tzu). Confucius lived in China more than two thousand years ago. He felt that the way to a good life was to create harmony between people. He wrote down many rules for people to follow in their relationships with one another.

16

Confucius thought that when people knew how to act and how to treat one another with proper respect, everyone would live in peace and harmony. He taught people to follow what we now call the Golden Rule. He said: "Do not do to others what you do not want them to do to you." The most important thing to learn in life, taught Confucius, was how to live and get along with others. Confucius did not talk about God or gods. When he talked of following "the Way of Heaven," he meant leading a good life, being a good person. The teachings of Confucius are known all over the world and are still considered to be very important ideas. These Chinese philosophies, or ideas about life, are often thought of as religions. Many people in China and other places live by these sets of ideas and beliefs.

Confucian scholars discussing proper behavior

Another set of important ideas came from India. Hinduism, one of the world's oldest living faiths, began in India more than four thousand years ago. Beliefs from the old nature religions, along with ideas from the many wise men who sang and chanted beside the banks of India's sacred rivers, formed the roots from which Hinduism grew. Hindus believe both in one supreme God and in many gods. To a Hindu, the idea of a Supreme Being, or God, is contained in Brahman, the eternal spirit or World Soul.

This statue of the god Shiva, dancing within a circle of fire, symbolizes the timeless cycle of creation, destruction, and rebirth.

The goal of Hindu life is to reach enlightenment—the highest level of understanding and wisdom. A Hindu seeks to become one, or join, with Brahman by following the many paths to God. Through self-control, purity, and charity, a person can turn away from the cares and suffering of the everyday world and achieve total peace and happiness. Hindus believe that each person's soul—the spiritual part that lives on after death—is continually reborn. The quality of the next life is determined by one's karma, or the total of all the good and bad in previous lives. The cycle of birth, death, and rebirth never ceases until Hindus accomplish the goal of enlightenment. Then they will rise above the everyday world to be rewarded by everlasting peace with Brahman.

Hindus recognize more than three hundred million gods and goddesses. Each represents one aspect or part of the supreme God, Brahman. The three most important gods are Vishnu, the Preserver, who sustains or supports all life; Shiva, the Destroyer, who makes room for new life; and Brahma, the Creator of all life. These three represent the most important aspects of Brahman. The wives and children of the gods are also highly revered. Vishnu's wife, Lakshmi, is worshiped as the goddess of good luck and fortune. Shiva's wife, Parvati, is also known as Kali and Shakti.

Karttikeya

Ganesha

Hanuman

The home is an important place for prayer in Hindu life. Although there are temples and large shrines for worship, Hindu families often have small shrines in their homes for their personal gods and goddesses. Offerings of food, drink, and gifts are placed at the shrine during prayer.

Hinduism has a rich tradition of religious art and writing. The many sacred books contain hymns, scriptures, poems, and stories. Epic stories about the heroic adventures of their gods and goddesses have long given Hindus inspiration and hope for their own lives. Today, there are more than six hundred million Hindus worldwide.

About twenty-five hundred years ago, in India, a young Hindu man, Siddhartha Gautama, gave the world another very important set of ideas. He was deeply dissatisfied with the answers he found in Hinduism and for six years he wandered alone, fasting and listening to holy men. Finally, after forty-nine days of meditation, or thinking very deeply, he found the answers he sought. These answers did not come to him while he lived a life full of worldly goods and pleasures. The answers did not come when he followed Hindu wise men, punishing himself by going without food and sleep. Instead, Truth and Knowledge came to him when he did neither. By avoiding either extreme, by rejecting both pleasure and pain, Gautama found the Middle Way.

Gautama found Enlightenment while meditating under a fig tree, now called the bodhi *or Tree of Wisdom.*

Buddha's first sermon to his disciples is often pictured in sculpture.

By following the Middle Way, Gautama found Truth and reached Enlightenment. He became known as the Buddha, or Enlightened One. The Buddha spent the next forty-five years of his life preaching to others about what he had learned. The Buddha did not talk about God or gods. Instead, he spoke of Truth as the way to salvation, or release from suffering. Through meditation, and following the Middle Way, one can know the Truth and reach Nirvana. Nirvana is a state of mind where one can find total peace and joy. Nirvana is salvation and the goal of all Buddhists.

The Buddha taught that in order to reach Nirvana, one must accept the Four Noble Truths: Pain and suffering are part of life; Pain comes from greed and wanting; Suffering will end when one is no longer greedy; The way to end all suffering is to follow the Eightfold Path. These rules for behavior teach that a person must have certain "right" attitudes and conduct in order to reach Enlightenment. These include always speaking both kindly and truthfully, never harming living things, thinking clearly, being alert, and meditating to seek the Truth.

Young Thai monks, with their begging bowls, wait for some rice.

Buddhist temples

Tibet

North India

Japan

In Buddhism, salvation comes from within. Each individual must reach Nirvana through his or her own efforts. Today, there are about three hundred million Buddhists in the world, living mainly throughout Asia. Many Buddhists still follow the ways of the Buddha, living a simple life of meditation and good deeds. Many other Buddhists follow another form of Buddhism in which the Buddha is revered as a godlike, divine being. These Buddhists believe that one can reach Nirvana and be saved through faith and total devotion to Buddha. But all Buddhists have the same high ideals: tolerance toward all, nonviolence, and respect and love for all living things.

Both Hinduism and Buddhism began in India. Another important world religion, Judaism, began in the Middle East about four thousand years ago. Judaism began with the story of a man named Abram, later called Abraham. Abraham grew up following the religious customs of the time, worshiping many gods and praying to clay and wooden images of these gods. But Abraham gradually began to think that it was wrong to worship in front of idols, that the true God could not be represented by a statue. He came to feel deeply that there was only one God, *the* God who should be respected and obeyed above all others. He put all of his faith and trust in this one, all-powerful God. The practice of monotheism began with Abraham's belief in one God and only one.

At first, Abraham's faith was practiced only by his close family, but over many years, his beliefs were accepted by all his people. Abraham's simple faith became a way of life for these ancient Hebrews, who would later be called Jews. This was the beginning of Judaism, from which in time would come two other great world religions—Christianity and Islam. Jewish history tells of a covenant or agreement between Abraham and God. If the Hebrews followed the laws of God, they would be rewarded for their faith and obedience. They were promised a land where they could live in freedom—the Promised Land, the land where Israel stands today.

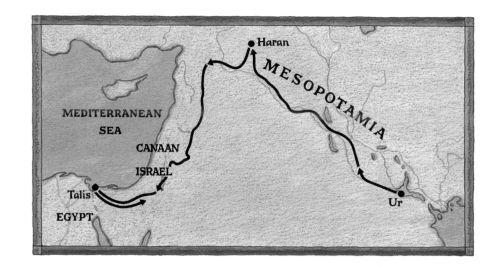

Abraham's migration took him from Ur to Haran. It was there, according to Jewish history, that God spoke to Abraham and promised him and his descendants the land of Canaan.

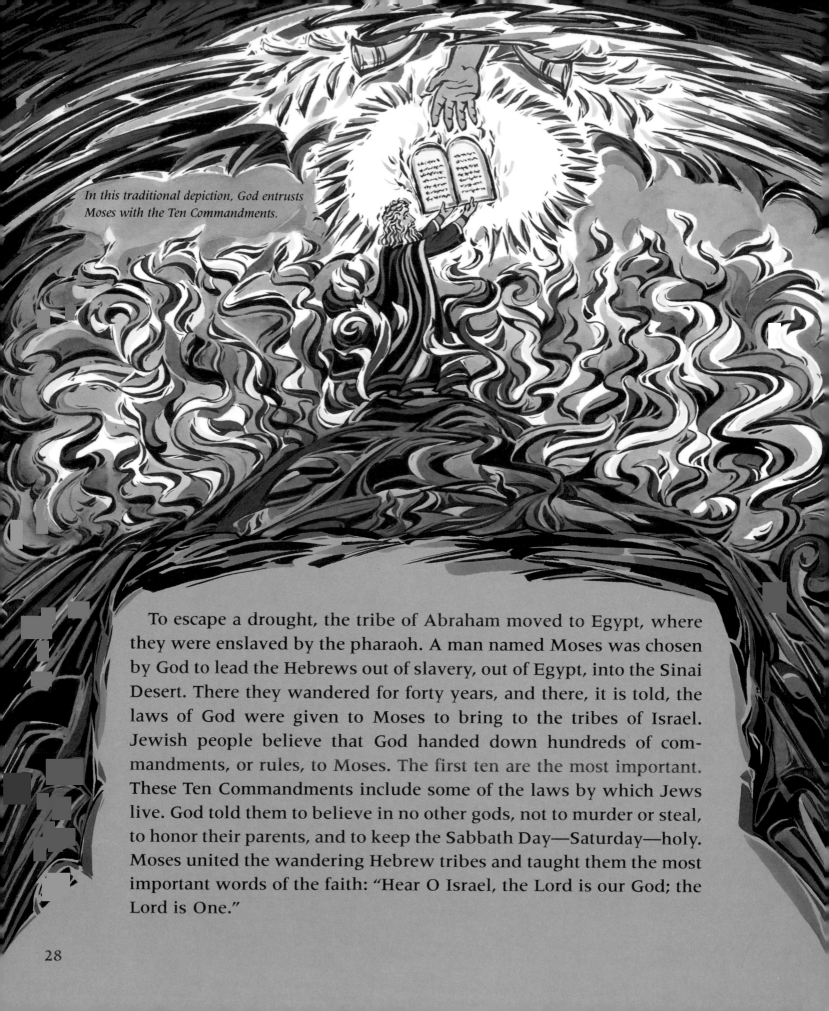

In this traditional depiction, God entrusts Moses with the Ten Commandments.

To escape a drought, the tribe of Abraham moved to Egypt, where they were enslaved by the pharaoh. A man named Moses was chosen by God to lead the Hebrews out of slavery, out of Egypt, into the Sinai Desert. There they wandered for forty years, and there, it is told, the laws of God were given to Moses to bring to the tribes of Israel. Jewish people believe that God handed down hundreds of commandments, or rules, to Moses. The first ten are the most important. These Ten Commandments include some of the laws by which Jews live. God told them to believe in no other gods, not to murder or steal, to honor their parents, and to keep the Sabbath Day—Saturday—holy. Moses united the wandering Hebrew tribes and taught them the most important words of the faith: "Hear O Israel, the Lord is our God; the Lord is One."

The words of the Torah scroll are hand-lettered in Hebrew.

הלכות מטמא
משכב ומושב

There are about seventeen million Jews living all over the world today. Although they live in many different lands and cultures, and although they do not all practice Judaism in the same way, they share the basic beliefs of the faith. They believe in one, everlasting God. They believe that God cares deeply for his people, and that they must respect and follow God's laws. Jews believe that loving God means loving one another and that God will judge people by their good deeds toward others. As they have studied the laws of the Hebrew Scriptures—the Torah—and the teachings of their faith, Jews have always believed in a better future. They look forward to a time when the Messiah, God's messenger, will arrive to unite the world in peace and love under the laws of God.

The sound of the shofar (ram's horn) announces the Jewish New Year.

Changes in thinking and new ideas are often brought to people by one special person. Confucius, the Buddha, Abraham, and Moses all had the ability to lead others and to communicate their ideas in a strong way. About two thousand years ago, another great leader began to teach and preach to others in Galilee, which was then part of the Roman Empire. He was a Jewish man, Yeshua, who became known as Jesus of Nazareth.

Many Jews lived in this part of the Middle East, and Jesus felt that some were not following the laws of God. As he traveled around, he spoke to them of the need to change their ways and to ask God for forgiveness. Jesus believed that sinners, those who did not live by God's laws, could not enter the Kingdom of the Lord after death. He thought that it was not enough just to agree to believe in God and his laws. To enter God's Kingdom, one must live God's Word through kindness and love.

Everywhere Jesus went, he attracted huge crowds. People loved to hear him speak. Soon he had many followers, including a number of Jewish men who became his disciples. Jesus preached to Jews and to Gentiles, or non-Jews. As he became more and more popular with the common people and spoke of ideas that went against the practices of the time, some Jewish religious leaders and the Romans who ruled the area began to fear Jesus. They were afraid of his power with the people and they turned against him. Many of his followers believed that Jesus was the promised Messiah, sent by God to bring peace and salvation to all. Later, some believed that he was actually the son of God. The Romans were afraid that Jesus would stir up trouble among the people under their control.

People gathered to hear Jesus speak.

Enemies conspired against Jesus. He was betrayed by a follower, tried by a high court of Jewish priests, and executed by the Romans. At that time, Roman execution was carried out by crucifixion. So Jesus was nailed to a cross to die alongside convicted criminals. It is what happened after the death of Jesus, however, that led to the acceptance of his teachings as a new religion called Christianity. His followers believed that on the third day after his execution, Jesus was resurrected, or rose from the dead. Even more people now came to believe that Jesus was the son of God—the true Messiah. He became known as Jesus Christ, from the Greek *Khristos*, meaning the Anointed One or Messiah. Christian religion revolves around events that make up the life, death, and resurrection of Jesus Christ. Important celebrations such as Christmas and Easter mark the birth and resurrection of Jesus.

Today, one-third of the world's population practices some form of Christianity. More than a billion and a half people all over the world share the basic beliefs of the Christian religion. They believe in one God, they believe that Jesus is the Messiah and the Son of God, and they believe that Jesus rose from the dead to give all people the promise of eternal life. Christians believe that those who lead a good life, loving God and other people and following what the Bible teaches, will be rewarded in Heaven with eternal life, while sinners will be punished in Hell. Although there are many groups of Christians—Roman Catholics, Eastern Orthodox, and numerous Protestant sects with differing beliefs and practices—they are all united in their faith in and love of Jesus as the Son of God.

A Protestant church

A Catholic cathedral

Just as Christianity grew out of Judaism, another of the world's great religions stems from both Judaism and Christianity. Islam began with the prophet, or teacher, Muhammad about six hundred years after the death of Jesus. In the area where Muhammad lived, in the Middle East, Arab tribes worshiped many gods. Muhammad, like both Abraham and Jesus before him, was disturbed by the way people were living—not caring for one another or for their gods. He began to think that the Jews and Christians he had met were right: that their God was the one true God. Like Buddha and Jesus, Muhammad spent time alone, meditating. After a while, he believed that he was visited by the archangel Gabriel. Through Gabriel, God's Truth was gradually revealed to Muhammad, who in turn brought this Truth to the world. People who accept Muhammad's message are called Muslims, or those who give themselves to God. The word *Islam* means "submission to God," or to Allah, the Muslim name for God.

The archangel Gabriel, as portrayed in a Turkish manuscript. Islam forbids pictures of Muhammad.

A Qur'an that has been lettered and decorated by hand.

Muhammad believed that he was chosen by God to be a prophet or holy messenger, just as Adam, Noah, Abraham, Moses, and Jesus were chosen before him. But he believed that he was chosen as the last prophet to bring the final and truest word of God to the world. Muhammad is thought to have received these revelations through Gabriel over a period of more than twenty years. These messages from God, as recited by Muhammad, make up the Qur'an (Koran), the holy book of Islam. Muslims believe that it contains the exact words of God and is a copy of the original book in Heaven. Biblical stories of both Jews and Christians are included in the Qur'an.

This Kufic script is one of the earliest written forms of Arabic.

35

An Islamic mosque

   The words of the Qur'an and the moral teachings of Muhammad are sacred to all Muslims. Islam is a way of life for nearly one billion people living throughout the world. Muslims live by Six Articles of Faith: They believe in Allah as the creator of all things; they believe in angels who record the good and bad deeds of every Muslim; they believe in the holy writing of the Qur'an; they believe in the prophets—Muhammad and those who came before him; they believe in a Day of Judgment—the last day of the world when all will be judged by their deeds; and they believe that those who have lived a good life will be rewarded forever in Paradise, while those who are evil and do not have faith will burn in Hell. Muslims also believe that the fate and future of each person are determined by the Will of Allah.

Muslims pledge their submission to Allah with the following words: "There is no other God but Allah and Muhammad is His Messenger." Muslims have five sacred duties to perform as part of their religion: They must recite the creed, or words of the faith; they must pray five times every day at certain hours; they must help those in need by paying a special tax to assist the poor; they must fast between dawn and sunset during the ninth month, Ramadan; and all Muslims should, at least once in their lives, make a pilgrimage to Mecca. This holy city, in Saudi Arabia, contains Islam's most important shrine—the Kaaba, which holds a huge black stone, a meteorite, believed to have come from God. Every Friday, Islam's holy day, Muslims gather in their mosques to kneel and pray. They turn to face Mecca and pledge themselves anew to Allah, their only God.

In the evening, thousands of worshipers surround the Kaaba at the center of Mecca's Great Mosque.

In today's world, the Chinese philosophies, Hinduism, Buddhism, Judaism, Christianity, and Islam are called the great world faiths. This is because they have existed for a very long time and because so many people practice these faiths in an organized way. But there are many other religions and belief systems in this world. They all influence the way people think and live their lives.

All over the world, there are groups of people who still practice the oldest forms of religion—tribal faiths, close to nature with devotion to many gods and spirits.

The figure of the Corn Mother represents the spirit of the Earth to many Native Americans in the southwestern United States.

Australian aborigines express their connection to nature through their art.

Many people practice more than one religion. In Japan, Shinto, an ancient nature religion, is followed hand in hand with Buddhism. In China, for centuries, people have lived by the ideas of Confucianism, Taoism, and Buddhism all together.

There are countries in the world where almost all the people belong to one religion. Islam is the religion of most of the people in many countries of the Middle East. In other countries, people belong to many different religions. In India, Hindus and Buddhists, as well as Jains, Sikhs, Muslims, and Zoroastrians, all try to live together, following their own religious faiths. In the United States, there are more than two hundred different organized religious groups, each with its own beliefs and practices.

Not everyone practices a religion or believes in a God or gods. There are about a billion people in the world today who are not part of any organized religious group. Some are atheists or nonbelievers. Many more are nonreligious—some are agnostics, unsure about God's existence, while others believe in a God or gods but do not practice any organized religion.

This Shinto shrine has the traditional gateway called a torii, even though it is on an island.

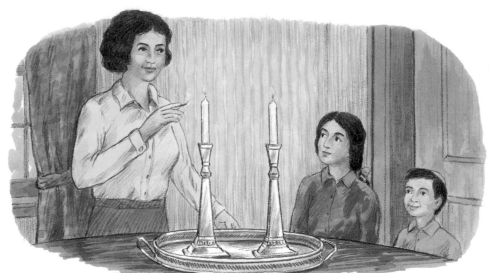

A Jewish mother lights the Sabbath candles.

There are many different ways of thinking and looking at the world. There are hundreds of answers to the questions that humans have wondered about since the beginning of time. The beliefs held by each religion or faith represent the answers or the Truth for the members of that group. The answers are not the same from group to group: The right answers or the Truth for Buddhists are not the same as the right answers or the Truth for Muslims. What is right for one person may not be right for another. Usually, religious beliefs come from one's family. A Hindu family will bring up children in the Hindu faith. A Jewish family will raise children with the beliefs of Judaism.

Oil is poured into lamps at a Buddhist temple.

Muslim children in Africa study verses of the Qur'an written on prayerboards.

Diversity of thought makes the world an interesting place to live in. Although people have many differing beliefs, they also have a great deal in common. The strong feelings that people have inside about God and the fulfillment that they get from the practice of their faith are very much the same throughout the world. Even though people call God by different names, read different holy books, and recite different prayers, many of their most important ideas are remarkably alike.

Young Sikhs learn to play the melodies of hymns.

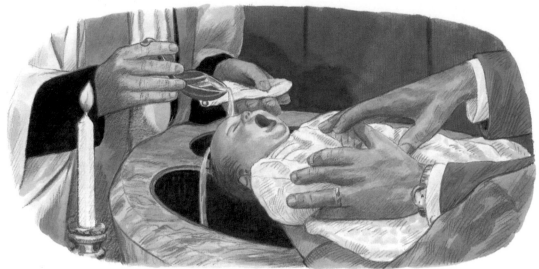

Baptismal water is poured on a baby's forehead in a Catholic church.

Most religions share certain ideas and customs. A belief in immortality, or life after death, is common to most faiths. Worship and prayer—whether formal or informal, at home or in a shrine, temple, or church—is universal, a part of every religion. Most of the world faiths have ceremonies or rites that are performed at important times in human life—birth, coming of age, marriage, and death. Throughout the world, people of all religions celebrate the special holidays and observances, both festive and somber, that stem from their beliefs. Most of the world's people believe in the Golden Rule and include it as part of their code of behavior. The idea of people treating others as they would wish to be treated is very much a part of most religious philosophies. Dealing with joys and sorrows through love and faith is part of the everyday practice of all the religions of the world.

Hindus bathe in the sacred waters of the Ganges River.

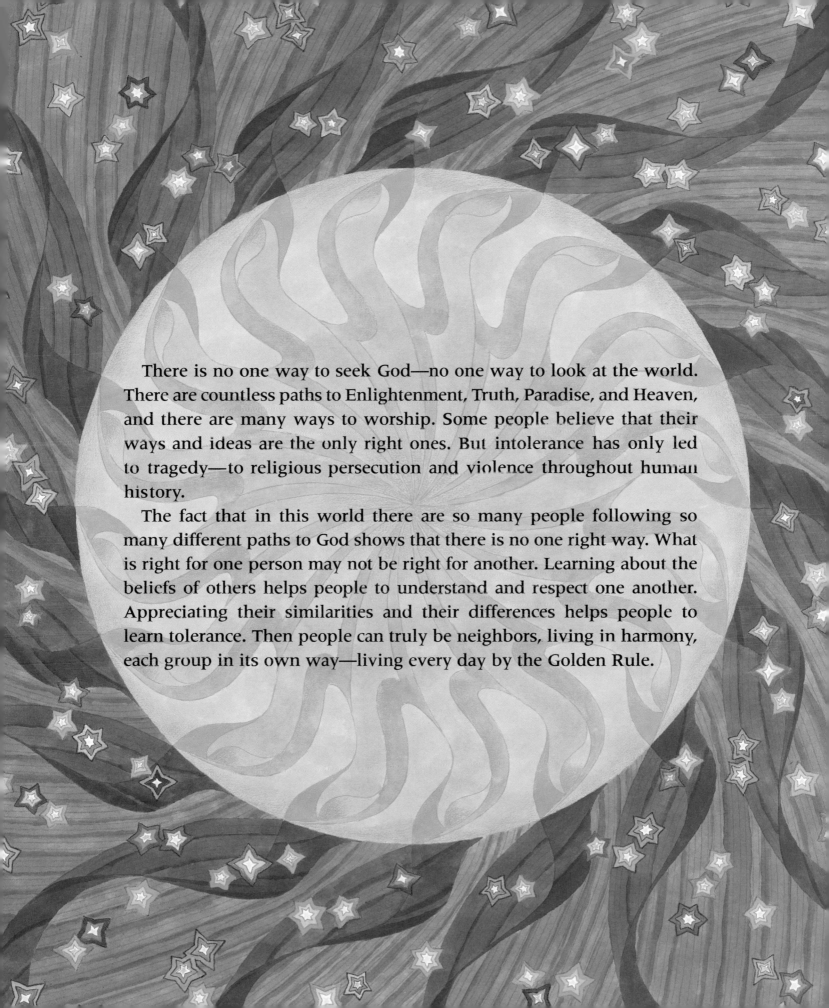

There is no one way to seek God—no one way to look at the world. There are countless paths to Enlightenment, Truth, Paradise, and Heaven, and there are many ways to worship. Some people believe that their ways and ideas are the only right ones. But intolerance has only led to tragedy—to religious persecution and violence throughout human history.

The fact that in this world there are so many people following so many different paths to God shows that there is no one right way. What is right for one person may not be right for another. Learning about the beliefs of others helps people to understand and respect one another. Appreciating their similarities and their differences helps people to learn tolerance. Then people can truly be neighbors, living in harmony, each group in its own way—living every day by the Golden Rule.

MORE ABOUT THE WORLD'S RELIGIONS

The Sacred Books

Confucianism: The Analects

The Analects is a collection of the selected sayings of Confucius, put together after his death. It is only one of four books that contain the teachings of Confucius, but is considered by many to be the most important and is certainly the best known.

Hinduism: The Vedas

There are four Vedas, made up of hymns and verses containing the main teachings and beliefs of Hinduism. The Rig Veda, the oldest, has ten thousand verses in a thousand hymns. The Upanishads, the last books of the Vedas, contain teachings about Brahman and writings about the other Vedas. The Puranas (myths) and two epic poems, the Mahabharata and the Ramayana, are also part of the sacred literature. The Mahabharata is the longest poem in the world and contains the popular and beloved Bhagavad Gita (Song of God).

Buddhism: The Tripitaka or Pali Canon

"The Three Baskets" of Buddhist Law contain the teachings of the Buddha in the Dhammapada, rules for monks and comments about the teachings. There are thirty-two books in all. Different Buddhist sects use different versions of the texts, some written in Pali and some written in Sanskrit (both ancient languages). The Sutras and Jataka Tales also relate the teachings of the Buddha.

Judaism: The Tanakh

The Tanakh is made up of the Pentateuch or Torah, which contains the Five Books of Moses, the Prophets (Nevi'im), and the Writings (Kethuvim). The Tanakh is the same as the Old Testament of the Christian Bible. The Talmud contains many volumes of discussion and interpretation of Jewish Law. These teachings of scholars and rabbis help to apply the laws to real life.

Christianity: The Bible

The Bible is made up of two books: the Old Testament, which is the same as the Jewish Tanakh, and the New Testament. The writings of the Old Testament tell the story of the Creation and give the history of the religion shared by Christians and Jews up to the time of Jesus. The New Testament is made up of writings by Christians in the first century A.D. They relate the teaching, life, death, and resurrection of Jesus Christ as told by his followers and disciples. The Apocrypha is made up of Jewish writings that are not in the Old Testament but are included in some Christian Bibles.

Islam: The Qur'an

The Qur'an (Koran) sets out the Word of God as told to Muhammad. It contains rules and laws for every aspect of human life. There are one hundred fourteen suras or chapters, meant to be recited aloud. The word *Qur'an* means "recitation" in Arabic. This sacred text is considered perfect only in its original Arabic, so any translation is inadequate. Many Muslims can recite the Qur'an from memory.

Other Sacred Texts

Zoroastrianism: The Avesta

Shintoism: Kojiki

Baha'ism: Kitab Akdas (or Kitabal-Aqdas)

Taoism: Tao Te Ching

Sikhism: Adi Granth

Jainism: Siddhanta

Festivals and Holidays

All of the world's religions commemorate special days and events. Some are marked by festive celebrations while others are somber and serious occasions. Here are some of the more important festivals and holidays.

Confucianism: The birthday of Confucius is celebrated with visits to his tomb. In temples, paper speeches are burned. It is believed that the smoke will carry good wishes to him in Heaven. The Chinese New Year is celebrated each year with a big parade and offerings to the gods. Paper dragons frighten away evil spirits to ensure a good harvest and good luck for the coming year.

Shintoism: There are four hundred matsuri or festivals each year, with processions and fairs at shrines all over Japan. Festivals take place at harvest and planting time, and when the cherry trees blossom. Some festivals have huge parades with many floats. People from all over Japan come to watch the beautiful celebrations.

Hinduism: There are many festivals during the year. Three of the most important are Dussehra, a ten-day celebration in honor of Kali, held in the fall; Divali, a festival of lights to mark the return of Rama to his kingdom; and Holi, a spring festival dedicated to Krishna. On these holidays, there may be feasting, dancing, and gift-giving. Divali also marks the New Year and is a time for new beginnings.

Buddhism: The festivals and holidays differ greatly from country to country. Wesak marks the birth of the Buddha. Houses and streets are decorated and generous offerings and gifts are given to Buddhist monks and to the poor. It is a time for Buddhists to rededicate themselves to following the teachings of the Buddha.

Judaism: There are many important holy days in the Jewish year. Rosh Hashanah is the Jewish New Year, a time to return to God and to think about sins committed in the past year. On Yom Kippur, the Day of Atonement, Jews fast and pray for forgiveness for their sins. Hanukkah is a festival of lights, commemorating the rededication of the temple in Jerusalem after its occupation by the Syrians. Passover, in the spring, celebrates the Exodus and the deliverance of the Hebrews from slavery in Egypt.

Christianity: The most important holidays in the Christian year celebrate the birth, death, and resurrection of Jesus Christ. Christmas marks the birth of Jesus in Bethlehem. The crucifixion and death of Jesus are remembered on Good Friday, which is a solemn occasion. The most joyous day of the Christian year is Easter Sunday—the time of the resurrection of Christ. Christians often observe a period of fasting and sacrifice during the forty days of Lent that precede Easter.

Islam: The most holy days on the Muslim calendar mark the important events in Muhammad's life that brought the Word of Allah to the people. Laila Al-Bar'h, or the Night of Forgiveness, is a time to forgive all old grievances and to prepare for the month of fasting. During Ramadan, the ninth month of the Muslim calendar, Muslims fast from sunrise to sunset each day. This marks the time when the Prophet began to receive the revelations from God. Dhu Al Hijja is the Month of Pilgrimage, a time when many Muslims make the journey to Mecca.

Some Other Religions

Zoroastrianism is a religion of ancient Iran and of Parsis. Followers believe in One True God—Ahura Mazda. Good and Evil are in constant battle and each person must choose Goodness to be rewarded in Paradise, where the body will be reunited with the soul in eternal joy. Life must consist of good deeds. There are about 500,000 Parsis in India today.

Jainism is a religion of India, related to Hinduism. Jains do not believe in one Supreme Power, but in the idea that every soul is a deity. Jains believe in a life of complete nonviolence and vow not to kill any living thing. They believe in rebirth—the soul may be reborn one million times. Self-control is essential to live a life free from emotion and full of compassion and kindness toward others. There are more than three million Jains.

Shintoism is a religion of Japan. Its name means "Way of the Gods." Thousands of Kami or spirits are worshiped. Worship and rituals have developed from an ancient nature religion. Worship may be at home or in a shrine, where a priest may conduct prayers. Small offerings or sacrifices are made to the Kami of the shrine. The Kami may be a natural object like a rock or tree, a divinity like the sun goddess, or a legendary person. Many Japanese practice both Shinto and Buddhism. There are more than three million Shintoists.

Sikhism is a religion of India that is related to both Hinduism and Islam. Sikhs believe in One God, Eternal Truth, which is everywhere and in everything and dwells within each person. They believe that God is merciful and that those seeking true knowledge of God will be granted peace, love, and union with God. Service in the temple and community is important in Sikh life. Males wear turbans and are known for their bravery and military skills. Sikhs number over sixteen million.

The Golden Rule

Since the time of Confucius, about twenty-five hundred years ago, the idea of the Golden Rule has been stated in many different ways. It has been part of the code of behavior in all of the world's major religions. Here are many different ways of expressing the same thought.

Confucianism: Never do to others what you would not like them to do to you.

Zoroastrianism: That nature alone is good which refrains from doing unto another whatsoever is not good for itself.

Taoism: Regard your neighbor's gain as your own gain, and your neighbor's loss as your own loss.

Hinduism: This is the sum of duty: Do naught unto others which would cause you pain if done to you.

Buddhism: Hurt not others in ways that you yourself would find hurtful.

Judaism: What is hateful to thyself, do not do to another.

Christianity: All things whatsoever ye would that men should do to you, do ye even so to them.

Islam: No one of you is a believer until he desires for his brother that which he desires for himself.

Index